Copyright © 2018 Bridget Irby All rights reserved.

No part of this publication may be reproduced, distributed, or transmitted in any form or by any means, including photocopying, recording, or other electronic or mechanical methods, without the prior written permission of the publisher, except in the case of brief quotations embodied in reviews and certain other non-commercial uses permitted by copyright law.

TABLE OF CONTENTS

DEDICATION 7
IMPORTANT NOTE FROM BRIDGET IRBY 11
YOUR FREE GIFT 17
First Commandment: Get Clear On The Mission 19
Second Commandment: Know Who You Serve 29
Third Commandment: Focus On What Matters First 36
Fourth Commandment: Know What You Believe 44
Fifth Commandment: Trust Yourself 48
Sixth Commandment: Set Yourself Apart 53
Seventh Commandment: Choose Your Mentors Wisely 59
Eighth Commandment: Choose The Right Strategy 65
Ninth Commandment: Avoid The Lies 73
Tenth Commandment: Forge Past The Fear . 80

YOUR NEXT STEPS 85
ABOUT THE AUTHOR 87

DEDICATION

*To my loving husband, our incredible children,
& the wise warriors who raised me…*

It is because of you that I am who I am.

For you, I am forever grateful.

<u>WARNING</u>

PROFIT INDUCING ACTIVITIES AHEAD

ENTER AT YOUR OWN RISK

IMPORTANT NOTE FROM BRIDGET IRBY

At some point in your life, things aren't going to go exactly as you plan.

This book is designed to make these times as infrequent as possible and to equip you with what you need to overcome them quickly when they do.

Inside this book, you'll find secrets that have taken me over a decade to learn.

Lessons learned from the trenches of business building…

In case you don't already know who I am, my name is Bridget Irby.

For the last decade of my life, I've been a student and teacher of all things marketing related.

I accidentally stumbled my way into the marketing world in 2007 and some would say, I found *"my gift."*

In my first year, with no marketing experience or background, I generated over 6 million dollars in revenue…

One might call it a fluke however, I went on to do it again…**six times…**in just a few short years.

Each company was not profitable when I started.

Each one became profitable within a short time of me being there.

I tell you this not so you think I'm incredibly special but because you should know, *I'm no different than you.*

I just know something that I think most people forget…something that is the foundation for success in anything you do.

Business isn't hard. It's <u>not</u> complicated. You don't have to *"hustle."*

You just have to solve problems.

People have problems that they are more than willing to pay to have solved. Each and every one of us wants to find the fastest, easiest way to our desired outcome — *whatever that may be*.

Your sole job as a business owner is to identify a problem *(that people are willing to pay to solved)*, solve it and communicate to your customers why they should choose you effectively.

It's really that simple.

Over our time spent together in this book, I'm going to share with you strategies and tactics anyone of which—*if applied*—can make you tremendously successful.

However, I want you to always remember that one thing—**business is simply solving problems**. Be on the lookout constantly for problems for which you can produce a solution quickly and easily.

The point of this book is to give you a set of business growth guidelines so you can grow your business successfully. My very own—*10 Commandments Of Business*—that you can quickly and easily reference when you need them.

If you know me, you know that I don't believe in wasting time.

Life is short and no one should spend it reading "fluff," so within these pages you'll find straight to the point advice and actionable insight.

To the same point, before we get started, I want to make sure you're in the right place.

This book is right for you if...
* You're starting a new business.
* You want to scale an existing business.
* You want to build a brand online.

If any of those are your goal, keep this book nearby and when you're in doubt or a problem has come up, reference the pages.

More than likely, you'll find the solution inside.

There is an important note that I want to make

before you dive in — the commandments aren't listed in order of importance.

They are all equally important. You cannot choose which ones to follow.

To be successful in business, you must follow them all.

Now, let's get started...

<u>YOUR FREE GIFT</u>

As my special gift to you for purchasing your copy of "Unleash Your Unstoppable Business," I'm giving you VIP access to **The Vault** for 30 days for free!

*Inside **The Vault** you'll discover…*

* *How to build a professional website for your business in just 60 minutes*
* *How to get beautiful graphics & logos made for just $5*
* *How to unlock your "it factor" by telling powerful stories that will captivate any audience*
* *Much, much more…*

The Vault is a one of a kind business-growth solution for entrepreneurs. Not only will you receive access to the on-demand how-to video training that you need with new trainings released every single month—you'll even have access to our team in a private member's-only Facebook group.

To get started, visit the site below today:

www.unleashtheunstoppable.com/gift

First Commandment: Get Clear On The Mission

If you don't know where you're going, how will you know when you get there?
— Steve Maraboli

Photo by Jens Lelie on Unsplash

Several years ago, we bought a house.

Not just any house though...

We bought a home that was more than twice the size of our previous home. It had a pool and tons of space. It was in a great neighborhood and an award winning school district.

It was also twice the price of our previous home.

We'd made the decision quickly and closed on the home less than two weeks after we saw it for the first time. We were so excited.

But...we quickly found that this house wasn't exactly the best fit for our needs.

We spent more time maintaining the pool than swimming in it...

We spent more time working than ever before because of the increase in note & utilities...

We had so much space that we rarely saw the kids & had that much more to clean...

Ultimately, we'd bought a home that wasn't at all what we wanted. Less than a year later, we were left wondering...where did we go wrong?

The answer—*we weren't clear on what we really wanted*.

Across the world, people are waking up today, making their coffee and silently wondering where they went wrong. For whatever reason, they are not where they want to be.

The only way to get what you want is to know exactly what that is.

*Do **you** know what you want?*

For this conversation, I'm not talking about cars or fancy houses — though those things are great and we have a few of each.

I'm talking about the kind of life you want in the long term.

Ultimately, it's the job of your business to support the kind of life that you want. In order to do that, you must be crystal clear on what you want.

Do you want to work 4 hours a day? Do you want to work 12 hours a day?

Do you want to be in one location or do you want the freedom to travel?
Do you want to just make enough money to get by or do you want to make millions?

The more specific you can be about the life that you want—the fastest you'll be able to create it.

Why?

Because so much of growing a successful business is about making the right decisions—each and every time. If you're clear on what you want, you have a filter to run each decision through.

Every time you have a decision to make, you simply ask yourself—"Is this in alignment with what I want to achieve?" If the answer is yes, go ahead. If the answer if no, don't.

So how do you uncover what you really want? **You can only find the right answer by asking yourself the right question.**

These are the three that I use with my clients:

1. **What type of life do I really want?**
2. **How can I either create a business or shift my current business to have that life?**
3. **What action steps do I need to take now to make that happen?**

4. Who do I need to become to make that happen?

We're going to dive into each of these questions in just a moment.

But first, I want to tell you why they are so important.

It's these questions that will allow you to create a business that you will love long term and one that will allow you to have what you want in life as well.

Begin with the end in mind and you will achieve your goal.

The end goal is never just a successful business. *The end goal is a business that supports the life & legacy you want.*

Now, let's unpack the questions.

These aren't easy questions to answer if you've never asked yourself them before so if you struggle at first, you're not alone.

Question One—What type of life do you really want?

When you answer this question, you want to dive deep and get as specific as possible. How many hours do you want to work? Do you want to manage employees? What bigger impact & legacy do you want to have? What do you want a typical day in your life to look like?

Dive deep here and do not hold yourself back. Like Oprah says, "In life, you get what you have the courage to ask for." The sky's the limit.

Question Two—How can I either create a business or shift my current business to have that life?

Now that you know what type of life you want, you can create a business that supports that life. If you want location freedom, you'll want an online business. If you want tremendous scale opportunity, you'll need a solid team to support you. What business model will best suit the kind of life that you want to have?

If you have a business in place already, how can

you shift that business to match what you want for your life? Do you need to hire someone to take your place in the company? Do you need to shift your products or services?

Question Three—What action steps do I need to take now to make that happen?

What specifically do you need to do in order have a business that supports what you want?

For example:

If you know that you need to hire someone, what's the first action that you need to do to start that process? Get clear on what that person will need to do every day. Write a job description. Post an ad. Interview. Hire.

If you know that your current prices don't support the income that you want, what's the first action that you need to take to raise your prices? Remove pricing from your website. Email your current customers.

Side note here on pricing: Make sure you know your worth & value. Don't undercharge.

Undercharging for your products or services doesn't do you or your clients any favors. If you can't be the lowest priced, there's no benefit in being second lowest.

I've had this conversation with my clients a lot. For most of my clients, I recommend doubling their prices and when I do, I typically hear…

"But Bridget, if I do that, I will lose half my clients!"

Yes...you will.

Double your prices. Lose half your clients.

Now you have half the work with the same amount of revenue.

Question Four — Who do I need to become to make that happen?

As business owners, we're constantly up-levelling. I can guarantee you to achieve the goals that you want to achieve, you'll have to become a higher and better version of yourself.

Be okay with that.

Evolving into a higher version of yourself is one of the best parts of life. We're learning and growing all the time.

Think about the kind of person who is already living the life that you want.

What are they doing differently on a daily basis than what you're doing right now? What do they know that you don't know? What do they do that you don't do? What are they not doing that you are doing?

When faced with a decision, ask yourself, "What would the person that I am becoming do in this situation?"

Knowing your mission means knowing what you want, what you need to do, and who you need to become to make it happen. This isn't something that you'll do once and never do again.

Your mission will grow and evolve as you grow and evolve.

If you don't take the time to stop and ask yourself these important questions, you'll never have the life or business that you really truly want.

When you do ask yourself the right questions, you'll be in the fast lane headed exactly where you want to go.

Second Commandment: Know Who You Serve

"Don't find customers for your products, find products for your customers."
— Seth Godin

Photo by freestocks.org on Unsplash

When you're a child, Christmas is a magical time.

The giant Christmas tree filled with freshly wrapped presents underneath and cookies for Santa Claus were the indicators that tomorrow would be the BEST. DAY. EVER.

One minute past midnight, it's time to open the

gifts and begin a day filled with family and fun.

It never fails though, somewhere wrapped up in pretty pink paper, is the gift from old Aunt Edna.

Aunt Edna means well.

Every year, she dutifully sends you a special gift. This year it's bunny socks.

What do you do with those bunny socks? They live someone in the back of your closet with the teddy bear sweatshirt that she sent you last year.

Pretty soon, the sweatshirt and the bunny socks will make their way to the local Goodwill.

Aunt Edna had the best of intentions so where did she go wrong?

She went out shopping and spent hours picking you out something that SHE thought would be great for you—something that she loved.

But here's the truth—without really knowing who you are and without asking you what you want, she can't possibly get you something that you actually want.

This is why her gifts have a short layover in the back of the closet on the way to their final destination—Goodwill.

What does this have to do with business?

Not knowing what their customer wants is the number one mistake that most business owners make. They build products and offer services that their customer wouldn't want *even if they were free*.

A CB Insights poll reports that up to 42% of starts up will fail simply because their market didn't want or need their products or services.

Why such a high number?

Because many businesses either lose touch with their customers' needs or they never even know their customers' needs to begin with.

You don't have to be one of those businesses. In fact, before you're finished with this chapter, you will know how to make your business bulletproof against this common mistake.

First, you have to get clear on exactly who you serve.

Who are your clients? Where do they live? How old are they? What problems do they have? What is their day to day life like? Where do they hangout?

These are all important questions that you want to be able to answer.

Next, you need to uncover what products or services you should offer to help them. You want to know answers like…

What do they want? What do they need? What problems are they having right now that they'd be willing to pay to have solved? How much would they be willing to pay for that solution? Do they have other problems that you can help them to solve?

You might be wondering how you get these answers...

Well...that's a little complicated.

Go ahead and get a pen and paper so you can take notes. I'll wait for you right here.

Okay, you ready?

Step One To Uncovering Everything You've Ever Wanted To Know:

Ask...

Really...that's it.

If you just ask people what they're struggling with, they'll tell you. People want help. They have problems that they need you to help them solve. They know they need help and they're willing to pay for it.

You can ask questions through phone calls, text messages, online surveys, focus groups—your options are truly endless. All you have to do is ask.

Here's where the magic happens:

When you know what problems they have...*you*

can identify ways you can solve them.

When you know what they're willing to pay for...*you can prevent yourself from ever building a product or launching a service that no one wants to buy.*

When you know how much they're willing to pay...*you can price your services appropriately.*

When you know what additional problems they're having...*you can create packages and bundles that will turn a one-time customer into a lifelong client. (The most expensive cost in most businesses is the cost to acquire a new customer so you want to encourage a long-term relationship with all your customers. This will sky-rocket your ability to scale.)*

When you know how your product or service will change their day to day life, *you can craft a marketing message which shows why they need you to reach their goal.*

When you know where they live, work, and play, *you can put that message in front of them to grow your business.*

If you consistently spend time getting to know what your customers want and need, you'll set yourself up for success in the long-term.

If you don't, you might end up selling something that people won't want *even if it was free...*

Third Commandment: Focus On What Matters First

"People think focus means saying yes to the thing you've got to focus on. But that's not what it means at all. It means saying no to the hundred other good ideas that there are."
— Steve Jobs

Photo by David Hofmann on Unsplash

When I was little I used to want to be a ballerina...but I'm short, chubby and a bit uncoordinated so that just was never really in the cards for me.

Instead, I would play ballerina — spinning around and around in my room. It never failed that after a few times of spinning I would lose my balance and fall down.

Several years after my first spin, a friend happened to see me take a spin and a tumble. Having the good sense that she has she recommended that I learn how to "spot" to keep my balance.

Little did I know...when a ballerina is spinning around and around a dizzying pace she uses a technique called "spotting" to prevent dizziness and complete their performance successful.

I gave it a try and sure enough...even I was able to spin and spin and spin.

So how does "spotting" work?

The ballerina focuses in a specific point in her field of view as she begins to turn. Each time she turns, her eyes go back immediately to focus on that same point. So instead of seeing the room spin, she's focused in on that one point.

This allows her to move rapidly, spinning again and again and again without getting dizzy or losing focus.

Learning how to "spot" in your business will be critical to your success as well.

As business owners, we're typically juggling a million and one things at any given moment.

It's easy to get distracted and when we're distracted, we can make the wrong decision, allowing the things that matter most to fall apart.

The more that your business grows, the more you'll have coming at you and the more you'll need to learn how to "spot" on the things that matter most.

The three areas that you must always have your eye on… **People. Profit. Products.**

Let's take a deeper look at each one of these.

People

Always be aware of what's going on with your market, your clients, and your employees. What does your market want & need? What do your employees want & need? What do your clients want & need?

I recently watched a very well-known influencer have a brutal fall from grace because they had lost touch with their market. They had a high tier group coaching program that they had hired someone to manage. That person had "managed" it so poorly that their initial stellar reputation was tarnished, clients were demanding refunds, and ultimately they lost trust with their market.

That's a hard pill to swallow and a humbling experience to say the least.

You can avoid situations like that by taking a few moments each day to focus in what matters. E-mail key clients and see how things are going. Talk to all your employees—not just senior level management. Stay in touch so you don't get caught by surprise.

Profit

If you're reading this book right now, I can almost guarantee that you're a visionary.

You're someone who has a lot of ideas and can quickly come up with strategies and business models. Chances are high, the people you surround yourself with are the same way.

Never lose sight of your profit margin.

Before you go chasing the next big thing, ask yourself—am I making what I want to be making in this business right now?

If the answer to that is no, figure out what you need to do to get there.

Don't be distracted by any shiny object. Keeping digging right where you're at until you hit the gold instead of starting a new hole.

If by any chance you've read this section while silently thinking to yourself, it's not about the money to me…

Please don't fool yourself.

I don't care how noble your mission is, you need money to make it happen.

No margin. No mission.

Focus on your profit.

You're running a business, not a charity.

Products

When I first started out in business, I knew that any money that clients were paying was good money because it was not *my money*.

The more experience that I gained, the more I came to understand that not all profit is created equal. For example, early on in my business, I offered my time for sell to anyone who needed any kind of marketing work. I had no minimum hours required—they could buy one hour or ten hours—and they could use that time for whatever they needed.

Because what I do is so specialized, it requires a full understanding of the clients business so I can provide appropriate support and recommendations from there. This, of course, takes a good amount of time.

What was happening is that even if clients purchased just one hour with me, I still had to spend several hours beforehand understanding their business, their problems, and what they wanted to achieve.

This bottleneck was killing my productivity and costing me loads of time and money. When I took away the one hour option and required a minimum retainer, my revenue shot through the roof, my frustration went away, and my client results increased.

Taking away that service allowed me to be more profitable, more effective, and less stressed.

I bet right now, you have a product or service offering that is costing you time, money and energy.

Find it.

Eliminate it.

Be on constant lookout for how you can streamline your products and services. Just like the ballerina, your world is spinning. Your "spot" point needs to be people, profit, and products.

If you do that, you can keep on spinning as long

as you'd like.

If you don't, you'll get dizzy and fall over before you know it.

Fourth Commandment: Know What You Believe

"Whether you think you can or think you can't, you're right."
— *Henry Ford*

Photo by Marjan Grabowski on Unsplash

On March 7th, 2017, we received the phone call that no parent ever wants to get. The chaplain at the local trauma hospital called us from our 18 year old son's phone. We didn't know the details, he just said to come as fast as we could.

When we arrived at the ER, we learned that our son had been involved in an accident on his motorcycle sustaining injuries that would change all of our lives forever.

For 37 days, he fought for his life in ICU as we listened to doctors tell us he was *never going to wake up...never going to walk...never going to talk...*

As much as we appreciated their opinions, we knew something that they didn't.

We know that our beliefs will guide our actions. We will behave in accordance with what we believe to be true.

We committed early on in that journey to believing and having faith that our son was going to get better. It was this belief that brought us through countless surgeries, a six month coma, failed procedures, emergency transfers and so much more.

You see, when you believe that your desired outcome is possible—you literally wire your brain to find a solution to any problem that comes up.

If you don't believe it to be possible, you wire your brain to find and focus on the problem.

Your brain is going to look for things that will prove your thoughts and beliefs to be right.

The year following his accident, we encountered countless problems.

For every problem, we chose to find a solution.

We refused to give up.

Ultimately that led to us moving our entire family to another state to have access to better medical providers, bringing our son home in a coma and commitment to caring for him 24/7 with feeding tubes & more so he didn't go to a nursing home, and leaving all our support behind in our hometown - all because we believed he would wake up and we were going to everything in our power to create an environment that encouraged that outcome.

The same thing is true for your business.

If you believe that you can have the business

that you want or the life that you want— you'll do everything in your power to create an environment to make that outcome possible.

If you don't, you'll silently sabotage yourself without even realizing it.

In case you're wondering...
6 months later our son woke up...
8 months later he took his first step…
10 months later he said his first word…
12 months later he could eat on his own...

NEVER. GIVE. UP.

Fifth Commandment: Trust Yourself

"The best place to find a helping hand is at the end of your own arm. — Swedish Proverb

Photo by Carl Heyerdahl on Unsplash

For many years, when I worked as an employee I was the "go-to" resource for corporate scale.

Every day, my phone would ring with business owners who had heard of my revenue generating abilities & wanted to recruit me to their teams.

Here is my secret confession…this constant flattery along with my consistent & easy results gave me a lot of confidence & pretty big head.

When I decided to go into business for myself, I carried that confidence and that big head right into business for myself. But...

Things weren't as easy as I thought they would be and slowly but surely, I began to lose my confidence. You see, I had a lot of experience in sales and marketing so generating clients wasn't a problem.

Building the systems in business and maintaining everything by myself was a whole new ball game. I struggled to juggle all the moving pieces and find the right people to support me.

I began to think there was something wrong with me and when that doubt began to creep in, I started looking for other people to tell me what to do. I just knew I must be doing something wrong.

My goal was to build a business online so I listened to the "gurus" and the self-proclaimed "experts." I did exactly what they told me to do.

I took course after course after course...

I started a blog...

I built a website...

I spent hours every day on social media...

For over a year, I spent 10+ hours a day learning and doing what these people told me to do.

Even when I didn't think it was right...

Even when I thought there was a better way...

Why?

Because somewhere along the way, I doubted myself and my ability.

Until eventually, I had enough. I was done working hard and I wanted to work smart. I decided to do things my way and when I did...*I built a six figure business from scratch in less than days.*

What changed?

I trusted myself.

I already had all the knowledge I needed and I had the one thing that no course could factor in — perspective on my own situation. I knew my strengths and my weaknesses so I just crafted a plan to play to those strengths and used what I already knew.

Have you ever heard the old fable about the devil's wedge?

The story goes that the devil was having a sale of his tools. On display were all his tools — jealousy, fear, and hatred — each with their own price tag. Standing alone on a pedestal was a worn and battered wedge. This wedge was the devil's most prized possession. With it alone, he could stay in business and for this reason, it was not for sale.

That wedge — the devil's most prized tool — was the wedge of doubt.

Hatred, jealousy, and fear may lead a person to

act unwisely...But the wedge of doubt could cause someone to do the worse thing of all... **nothing**.

It's easy to doubt yourself in business...

If you're doing it right, you mess up a lot. You fail your way forward not really knowing exactly what's right and what's wrong—that's okay.

When you stumble, get the support & knowledge that you need to grow.

Ultimately, trust in yourself that you can and will figure it out no matter what happens.

When you learn how to trust yourself no matter what happens, you will be able to fail your way forward—solving any problems as they arise—to create the business that you want.

If you don't learn how to overcome doubt, you'll be sitting still—a hopeless victim of the devil's favorite tool.

Sixth Commandment: Set Yourself Apart

"There is a way to do it better..find it."
—Thomas Edison

Photo by Andrea Tummons on Unsplash

A Girl Scout comes to your door to sell you Girl Scout cookies.

You LOVE girl scout cookies.

She's selling one box of cookies for $5, only takes cash, and it will be three weeks before delivery. You don't have any cash so she goes away empty handed.

A second girl scout comes to your door.

She's selling cookies for $5 a box but if you buy 10 boxes you get a box free. She takes credit cards and checks and will deliver in one week. You buy 10 boxes.

As you start to write the check, she asks you if you'd like to buy an extra ten boxes that you could freeze since they won't be for sale again for another year. Now, you buy 20 boxes.

Who wins?

The doctor...because now you have diabetes.

Just kidding.

Obviously, the second Girl Scout wins. First, she made it really easy for you to buy. Second, she offered you a more inclusive package. Third, she thought about your need for Girl

Scout cookies later in the year and made you an intelligent additional offer. In that scenario, you both win. You get Girl Scout cookies all year long and she has now sold 20 boxes instead of none.

That's what you should always strive for—the win/win situation.

When you strive for the win-win and serve your clients on a higher level, you'll always set yourself apart from everyone else.

Let's go over a few ways that you can set yourself apart.

Money Back Guarantee

Offering a money back guarantee helps to overcome one of the most powerful objections. It says that you believe so strongly in your product or service that they can try it with essentially no risk.

Bundling Options

Just like the second Girl Scout bundled cookie

boxes, you can bundle your services or products together. Think about what you're selling right now that people typically buy together. How would you create a package or bundle that would make sense for your business and your clients?

Extended Support

When you buy a computer at most stores, they'll immediately offer you an extended warranty. This offer will allow you additional protection and support if you need it. What services or products do you have right now that you could offer extended support on? The great thing about extended support in terms of business is that, when done right, it can provide for continuity revenue that you can count on.

For example: When we build a website for a client, we offer continued hosting as an extended support service. This means the client doesn't ever have to worry about their website. We take care of updates, security, and backups. The client pays a small monthly fee for the service. It's a win-win on both sides.

Fast Delivery

We live in a day and age where everyone wants something fast. What products or services could you get done twice as fast? Are people willing to pay for that speed?

In most cases, the answer is yes.

For example: We have a package that focuses on speed only. In 48 hours, our team will build an entire brand from scratch including website, logo, and social media profiles. Obviously this service is more expensive than our traditional builds because of the quick turnaround time but people use this service every day.

Convenience Services

How can you make buying from you more convenient? We've found that one of the barriers to many purchases is that people don't have extra time. They may want to get their oil changed but they don't have time. They want to go to read that book but they don't have time.

What can you do right now that would make

buying from you more convenient than buying from anyone else?

For example: An automotive shop could offer free drop off and pick up for services. An author could offer an audio book instead a print book so that people can listen on their way to work...think Audible.

Setting yourself apart will be crucial to your success in both the immediate and the long-term. Having these unique differences allows you to clearly answer the question - *Why would someone buy from you over your competitors?*

If you know the answer to that question, it makes choosing your business a simple choice.

If you don't, often times you'll walk away with all your Girl Scout cookies in hand.

Seventh Commandment: Choose Your Mentors Wisely

"Don't let the noise of others' opinions drown out your own inner voice."
—Steve Jobs

Photo by Jeff Nafura on Unsplash

I can remember getting ready to walk out the door on my first big trip as a teenager.

Just me and my 1988 Chevy Corsica headed to the beach for a few days of fun in the sun.

Back in those days, we didn't have GPS to guide our every move. I had, in fact, printed out a map from my computer and set out on the road.

Being all of 18 years old, I hadn't thought ahead to check the weather or book a hotel. I just printed my map, got in the car and drove. And like a genius, I'd left in the middle of the night.

One hour into my trip, I drove straight into a severe thunderstorm.

The wind whipped around, pushing the car from side to side. Lightning flashed across the midnight sky. I could hear trees breaking and falling to the ground under the force of the wind.

The rain was so thick I couldn't see the street signs anymore. One wrong turn led to another wrong turn until I was completely lost.

I pulled over at the first gas station I could find and rushed inside carrying my map. On my way inside, my map got soaked with the rain.

By the time I made it in, the ink on the paper had bled and been washed away. My map was unreadable.

I approached the counter. A boy my age was waiting for me there.

As much as he wanted to help, he couldn't give me directions to where I needed to go **because he didn't know how to get there.** It was someone he'd never been so he couldn't tell me how to get there.

It wouldn't have made sense for me to continue asking him questions—demanding that he give me an answer because his answer would be wrong.

Yet, as business owners and entrepreneurs, we sometimes do the same thing.

Have you ever asked your friends or family members—who have never owned a business—for advice on what you should do in *your* business?

That's like the blind leading the blind…

Would you ask someone who can't drive for

driving tips? No.

To get to where you want to go faster, you'll need a trusted advisor—to help you find your way.

Choosing the wrong person can lead to a lot of wasted time, money, and energy.

So how do you know who is qualified to help you?

Here are the questions that I recommend asking:

One—Have they accomplished what you want to accomplish?

We've already covered this a bit so I'm not going to harp on it. Don't ask people who have no experience in a particular area for advice… You'll just be left with bad advice.

Two - Do they really listen to you?

Good listening skills are CRUCIAL in a mentor relationship. If your mentor doesn't listen to you, they can't possibly know what you want or what you need. If you find someone who interrupts you or you don't feel like they understand you - run.

Three—What kind of support do they provide?

Before you go out in search of someone to help you, you need to know exactly what you want help with and what you want to achieve.
 Different people offer different types of support.

For example:

We are an all-inclusive agency offering business coaching, strategy consulting, and done for you services. This means that when someone starts with us, they can finish with us as well. If we help you identify your strategy, we'll help you execute it. You don't have to try to find people to help you execute Facebook™ ads or build your website. We are one of the few companies that handle it all.

This is important because if we just gave you a strategy and left, then you'd be searching around for developers, designers, and copywriters to help you execute your strategy.

So before you sign with anyone, make sure they offer the kind of support that you want.

Four — Are they willing to challenge you?

You want to know that your mentor is willing to challenge you when you're wrong or when you need some perspective. The relationship that you have has to be one of trust and confidence. If it's not, it's ineffective.

When you choose the right mentor to support you on your journey, you'll shave years off your learning curve.

If you don't, you'll end up stuck in the rain in the middle of nowhere.

Eighth Commandment: Choose The Right Strategy

"One size never fits all. One size fits one. Period."
—Tom Peters

Photo by NeONBRAND on Unsplash

A couple of weeks ago, I had a sales call with a potential new client. She owns a web development company and has been in business for a long time. Her only source of leads was her SEO ranking which had been wiped out by a competitor.

She went from having consistent leads & calls coming in to nothing.

She searched around for help desperately to get her SEO back on track but nothing could be done. When she figured that out, she went to work learning about marketing and implementing different marketing techniques.

By the time we got on the phone, she had invested over $30k and was literally no closer to a solution. In tears, she told me she felt like a failure.

All the people that she purchased courses and training from guaranteed that their process worked...meaning that it wasn't their "proven system" that was broken—it was her.

But she wasn't a failure and if you've experienced the same thing, neither are you.

She had the wrong strategy and she thought that what worked for someone else would work for her even though their business was very different.

Within 45 minutes on the call with me, she had a custom strategy outlined just for her business that played to her strengths and overcame her weaknesses.

You will not ever hear me promote a one size fits all solution.

Why?

Because they don't work.

You need to find the right solution for your unique needs and challenges.

For example:

If you're a great writer and you want a location independent business, blogging might be a great fit for you. You shouldn't waste your time trying to build a webinar or have a YouTube channel.

If you hate marketing and you have the cash to outsource it hiring a company to manage it for you will be your best bet.

Thinking that a 30 day video course without any human interaction is going to solve all your marketing problems is kind of like thinking that a one size fits all dress will look the same on everyone.

It's just not going to happen.

In the next few minutes, I'm going to go over two growth tactics that work in almost every business. How you apply them will be different depending on your strengths and weaknesses.

When you hit a bump in the road or need to increase your leads, come back here and see which of these two tactics you can quickly implement.

Strategic Partnerships

Strategic partnerships are mutually beneficial referral relationships. Think of a real estate agent and a mortgage lender. If you're buying a home, you'll need a real estate agent and chances are high, you'll need a mortgage as well.

It would make sense as a real estate agent to have a trusted mortgage lender to refer your client to so you know they are well taken care of and you get to work with someone you enjoy.

The same is true for a mortgage lender. They would want a trust agent to refer their customers for the same reasons.

By developing these partnerships, you can quickly double the amount of leads & referrals you're receiving while increasing the value for your clients.

There's no contract of formal agreement—just a simple referral relationship.

Make sense?

For a strategic partnership to be effective, it must meet several criteria:

1. You must have complimentary services or share the same type of client.
2. The potential partner must have a stellar reputation and provide excellence service.
3. You must actually enjoy working with them.

Some examples of strategic partnerships:

1. Doctor → Hospital

2. Web Developer → Web Designer
3. Dog Groomer → Veterinarian

What type of business would be a good strategic partner for you?

Side note: A variation of the strategic partnership is an affiliate relationship. In an affiliate relationship, you would find someone who has a similar audience to you and offer them a commission for selling your products or services.

Speak To Sell

The public speaking model is one of my favorites because if it's used appropriately is incredibly effective.

Now obviously, this isn't right for you if you hate public speaking. But even if you do hate public speaking, I'd recommend you push yourself sometime and give it a try. Remember, nothing good ever comes from your comfort zone.

So how do you speak to sell effectively?

Here's how it works:

1. Identify a speaking engagement that puts you in front of your ideal clients. (This means the people who will pay you to solve their problems.)
2. Deliver an incredible presentation sharing with them exactly what they should do to solve their problems.
3. Close your presentation with a soft offer to support them in executing what they should do. (You give the "what" in the presentation but the "how" is what they pay for.)
4. Have comment cards on each person's chair and tell them to fill out the cards to receive [relevant free gift] or to schedule a consultation.
5. Follow up with each lead and turn them into a raving fan.

What makes speaking so special is that it speeds up the buying process tremendously. Typically before someone buys from you, they must go through three phases.

Introduction → Trust Building → Purchase

So first, they must be introduced to your company and what you do. Then you have to spend time nurturing that relationship with them so that they trust you as a person and that you can solve their problems. Once you've done that, they must decide if they're ready to purchase.

The amazing thing about speaking is that when you step on stage — half the work is already done. You're on stage as a speaker which means that you have you borrowed trust and authority simply because you're on stage. During your presentation, you'll have the opportunity to demonstrate your expertise which will then allow them to trust that you can solve their problem. With a soft call to action at the end, they are primed and ready to buy.

If you learn how to implement these two techniques into your overall strategy consistently, you will never be at a loss for leads.

Want help identifying your own unique strategy? Apply for a free strategy call with our team at unleashtheunstoppable.com/apply

Ninth Commandment: Avoid The Lies

*"Don't be trapped by **dogma** – which is living with the results of other people's thinking."*
— Steve Jobs

Photo by Antonio Grosz on Unsplash

One of the greatest things I've seen people struggle with is the "herd mentality."

Herd mentality is when people act the same way or believe the same thing just because people around them believe or behave that way. Often, they ignore their own gut feelings in the process. Think of a sheep blindly following the flock no matter where they go just because that's what the **herd** is doing.

I've done it.

At some point, you've done it.

As an entrepreneur, you have to consistently be checking on and asking yourself what you believe. Because remember...your behavior will be in alignment with what you believe.

This chapter is all about setting straight some of the myths that many entrepreneurs believe, especially when it comes to growing your business or brand online.

In the next few minutes, we're going to tackle two of the most common lies that are so widespread that most people believe them to be truth. There are many more but I've chosen the two most prominent for this book.

Lie One—You have to have a huge list, a fancy website, and be active on every social media platform to grow your business or brand online.

When I first started out in business for myself, I wholeheartedly believed this. Which was strange since in all my days growing businesses and running teams in the corporate world, I never sent anyone to our website or social media.

Either which way, I did what the guru's said to do. I spent hours every day on social media. I built an incredible website. I put out a ton of content. And ultimately...I ended up with a HUGE reach on Facebook™.

My content was being shared a ton and over 70,000 people per week were viewing my posts. I knew at that point, I was ready to launch my first product — an online course.

So I set out to make the best online course ever. I spent hundreds of hours and thousands of dollars bringing it to life. I just knew when I launched it that people would line up to save their spot.

But...when launch day came...it was a very different scene.

No one came.

Even though they were sharing my content, liking my posts, and following me online—they didn't want what I had built. *(Think back to the bad gift from Aunt Edna…)*

So why didn't it work?

Because marketing and business growth is the same whether it's online or offline—it's all about connection. True real connection - where your clients and future customers know you, trust you, and understand that you can help them solve their problem.

And...Where you understand their wants and needs.

Having a website, a list, or a social media platform without true real connection is like having a beautiful car with no engine.

It's pretty to look at and it might make you feel good but it certainly won't get you anywhere.

Lie Two—People won't take you seriously as a professional without a certification.

"Oh, I can help you with that if you want..."

Those words fell right out of my mouth before I could overthink it and stop myself. I was standing in our home talking to an agent when she began sharing some of her frustrations at what she was struggling with online.

To me, it sounded like a simple fix so *before I could think*, I told her I could help her. She was excited about me helping her and looking forward to it.

But me...I was terrified.

As soon as those words came out of my mouth, I immediately began to doubt myself...

Do I really have what it takes?

I've never done this for someone else in this way before, how much do I charge?

What kind of agreement do I need?

Am I really qualified to help her?

It's funny how we do these things to ourselves. We think we need all these things that we really don't. You see, at that point in time, I already 7 marketing certifications specializing in digital media.

I was completely comfortable charging for my traditional marketing consulting but I never charged for social media management, website optimization, Facebook ads or content management. I felt panicked and scared, thinking I was not ready. So… was I ready?

Of course I was! Just like you are right now.

In just a few short months, I did for her what she had paid another company tens of thousands of dollars to do and after a year...they *still* didn't have it done. I saved her a ton of time, money and energy. Working with her gave me the confidence I needed to build the company that I have today.

Getting a certification will not give you confidence.

Getting results for your clients will.

Results = Certainty In Your Ability

Certainty = Confidence

If you're waiting to launch a product or service until you get certified *(in something you already know how to do),* listen up here—this is important.

Waiting to help your future clients and customers until you get another certification is like walking past someone who is drowning because you're not a certified lifeguard.

Would you let someone drown because you're not "certified" to save them?

No, you wouldn't. If you know how to swim and can safely get them out, you'd do it without thinking twice about it. Your instincts would kick in and you'd be the hero.

It's no different in business.

Stop holding yourself back. Be the hero.

Tenth Commandment: Forge Past The Fear

"Action cures fear, inaction creates terror."
—Douglas Horton

Photo by Austin Chan on Unsplash

"Absolutely, I would love to."

Again the words fell right out of my mouth before I had a chance to think about them. I had just accepted my largest speaking engagement without a second thought. *Perfect*.

No really—**that was perfect**.

Because if I had stopped to think about it, I probably would have gotten nervous and turned it down. Immediately doubt would set it in and I would start asking myself—*Am I really ready? Can I really do this?*

That's what happens when we stop to think too much. It's what holds so many business owners back time and time again. But what's the root cause?

FEAR

Fear of failure...

Fear of success...

Fear of judgment...

Fear of letting people down...

The list goes on and on.

In this final chapter together, I want to spend some time sharing with you the lessons that I've learned about fear. You have to understand first that fear is often disguised as rationality, procrastination, discouragement, and many other things.

If you know what you should be doing but you're not doing it, chances are high you have some fear in there somewhere that's holding you back.

Fear is good and bad. It's good because it's designed to protect us. Being afraid of heights is great because it can keep you safe from falling. But the way fear works, because it's a part of your primitive brain function, it doesn't distinguish between real threats (like dinosaurs and cliffs) and new things (like speaking engagements and new business opportunities.)

Your primitive brain will naturally perceive anything new as being potentially dangerous and therefore will make you fearful. But you have the power to overcome that fear.

How?

There's only one way to overcome any kind of fear...

ACTION

That's the secret that many people don't understand...you can take action *even when you're afraid*. You have the option to feel the fear then act anyway.

The fear is going to be there - it's not going anywhere. It's literally encoded in your DNA but...the more that you develop the habit of taking action even when you're afraid, the easier taking action in the face of fear will become.

Afraid of reaching out to potential clients because they might reject you? Send that email anyway.

Afraid of checking in with past clients that you haven't talk to in a while Make that call anyway.

If it's not going to physically harm you, *what do you really have to lose?*

Make sure that you keep things as simple as possible when faced with fear. Identify what is the one single action that you can take right now to move forward to achieve your goal.

If I know anything, I know this…

You have this one life.

That's it.

There are no do-overs.

No second chances.

It is entirely up to you to write your own story.

YOUR NEXT STEPS

Congratulations!

You are well on your way to your unstoppable business.

If you have any questions or would like to be supported on your journey, reach out to me at info@unleashtheunstoppable.com.

Oh, and don't forget to snag your free access of *The Vault* at unleashtheunstoppable.com/gift.

It's sure to skyrocket the growth of your unstoppable business.

See you there,
Bridget Irby

ABOUT THE AUTHOR

Bridget Irby is a sought-after speaker, branding strategist, and marketing trainer. With over 10 years of experience. She leads a team of Facebook™ Ad Experts, Designers, and Developers to grow brands all over the world.

Outside of business, she is a dedicated wife, mother, and a community leader.

Learn more about Bridget & her team any visiting the site below:

www.unleashtheunstoppable.com

Made in the USA
Lexington, KY
26 July 2019